How are cars made?   18

How are cars tested?   19

Which is the world's longest road race?   20

Where is the world's longest road?   20

What is a road train?   21

When were bicycles invented?   22

Which is the fastest motorbike?   23

Who built the first locomotive?   24

Which was the fastest steam train?   25

Which is the fastest electric train?   25

Where is the world's longest railway?   26

Where is the world's highest railway?   26

What are monorails?   27

Which are the biggest ships?   28

What were the first boats like?   30

How fast could sailing ships travel?   31

How do paddle-steamers work?   32

Who first sailed solo around the world?   33

Which is the fastest boat?   33

How do hovercraft hover?   34

What is a hydrofoil?   35

How deep can submarines dive?   36

What will future transport be like?   38

Useful words   39

Index   40

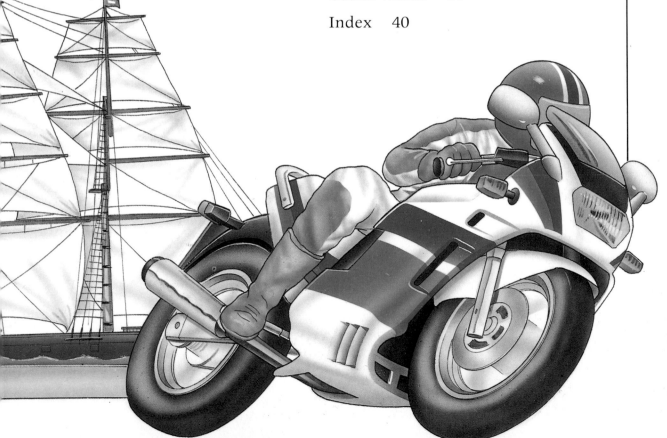

How fast can aeroplanes fly?

Faster and faster planes have been built since the first powered flights took place early this century. Today, the record for the world's fastest jet plane is still held by the USA's Lockheed SR-71A. In 1976, it flew at 3530 km/h.

The fastest planes in the world are those powered by rocket engines – only Space rockets can fly faster. In 1967, the USA's X-15 rocket plane flew at 7297 km/h!

DO YOU KNOW

The speed of sound slowly drops with height above sea level, but above about 11,000 metres it stays the same. It's around 1225 km/h at sea level, and about 1060 km/h above 11,000 metres. A plane flying at the speed of sound is at Mach 1. Twice the speed of sound is Mach 2, and so on.

The USA's X-15 (above) remains the fastest plane ever made. Its rocket engine propelled it to nearly seven times the speed of sound.

The first plane to fly faster than the speed of sound in level flight was the USA's rocket plane, the Bell X-1 (above), in 1947.

The jet-engined Anglo-French Concorde (above) is the world's only supersonic passenger plane. Its cruising speed is around 2330 km/h.

TELL ME ABOUT

WINGS
WHEELS
& SAILS

SERIES EDITOR: JACKIE GAFF

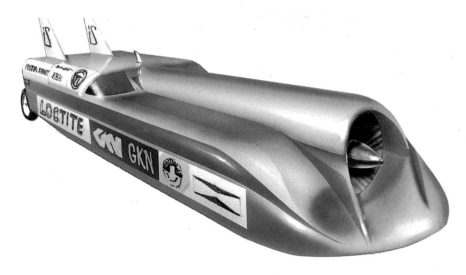

Kingfisher Books

Series editor: Jackie Gaff
Series designer: Terry Woodley
Author: Tom Stacy
Consultants: David Jefferis, Terry Jennings
Designer: David West Children's Book Design
Illustrators: Peter Bull (pp. 2–3, 8–13, 16, 18–19, 20 top, 22–3, 25 top, 26–7, 30–1, 33 bottom, 36–7); Tony Gibbons (pp. 17, 20 bottom, 21, 24, 25 bottom); Sebastian Quigley (pp. 4–7, 14–15, 28–9); Steve Weston (pp. 32, 33 top, 34–5, 38); Michael Roffe (p. 39).
Cover illustration: Ross Watton (Garden Studio)
Editorial assistant: Anne O'Daly

Kingfisher Books, Grisewood & Dempsey Ltd, Elsley House, 24–30 Great Titchfield Street, London W1P 7AD

First published in paperback in 1992 by Kingfisher Books
10 9 8 7 6 5 4 3 2 1
Originally published in hardback in 1990 by Kingfisher Books
Copyright © Grisewood & Dempsey Ltd 1990

BRITISH LIBRARY CATALOGUING IN PUBLICATION DATA
A catalogue record for this book is available from the British Library

ISBN 0 86272 616 6

Phototypeset by Southern Positives and Negatives (SPAN), Lingfield, Surrey
Printed and bound in Spain

Contents

How fast can aeroplanes fly? 4

Which is the biggest aeroplane? 6

Who flew the first aeroplane? 7

Who first flew around the world? 7

How do aeroplanes stay in the air? 8

How do gliders stay in the air? 9

How do helicopters fly? 10

What are V/STOL jets? 11

Why do balloons fly? 12

What are airships? 13

Which is the fastest car? 14

Which is the most popular car? 16

Which is the biggest car? 16

Who invented the motor car? 17

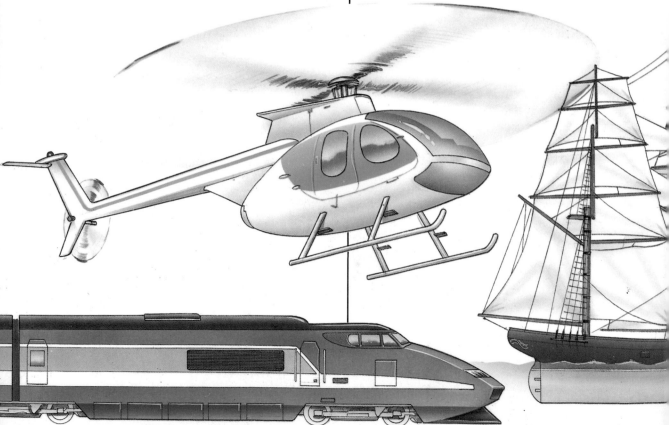

The USA's jet-engined spy-plane, the SR-71A Blackbird (below), could cruise at Mach 3 – that's three times the speed of sound.

Which is the biggest aeroplane?

The world's largest passenger plane is the USA's Boeing 747, or jumbo jet. It is 70 metres long and weighs over 400 tonnes. The heaviest plane is the Russian Antonov An-225, which weighs 508 tonnes.

JUMBO FACTS

● In 1989, a QANTAS Boeing 747-400 flew non-stop from London, UK, to Sydney, Australia, in a record 20 hours.

The body of a plane is called the fuselage. Inside the 747's fuselage is the passenger cabin, with seating for about 400 people.

The 747's wings measure 60 metres from tip to tip. The plane has four jet engines, mounted two beneath each wing.

The flight deck is where the captain and co-pilot sit. There is also an automatic pilot – a computer which can fly the plane.

PILOT'S CODE

Every plane has a code name made up of letters and numbers. So that no one mixes up the sounds, pilots use the sound alphabet shown here to give these names over the radio. You could use it to send messages in code to your friends.

A Alfa
B Bravo
C Charlie
D Delta
E Echo
F Foxtrot
G Golf
H Hotel
I India
J Juliet
K Kilo
L Lima
M Mike
N November
O Oscar
P Papa
Q Quebec
R Romeo
S Sierra
T Tango
U Uniform
V Victor
W Whisky
X X-ray
Y Yankee
Z Zulu

Who flew the first aeroplane?

The first person to fly a plane was Orville Wright of the USA, on 17 December 1903. People had flown in balloons and gliders before this, but Orville Wright was the first person to fly a plane with an engine.

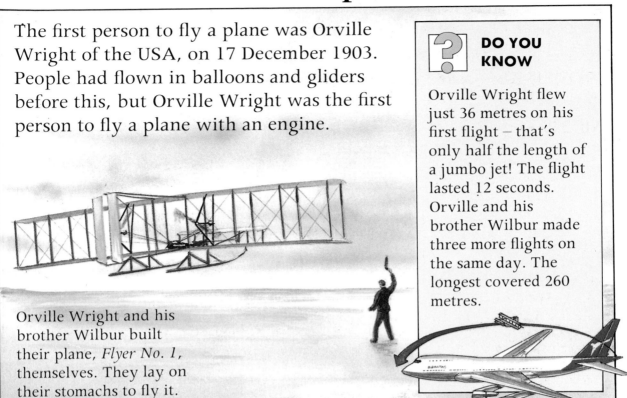

Orville Wright and his brother Wilbur built their plane, *Flyer No. 1*, themselves. They lay on their stomachs to fly it.

? DO YOU KNOW

Orville Wright flew just 36 metres on his first flight – that's only half the length of a jumbo jet! The flight lasted 12 seconds. Orville and his brother Wilbur made three more flights on the same day. The longest covered 260 metres.

Who first flew around the world?

The first planes to fly around the world were two US Douglas seaplanes in 1924. They took 175 days. US pilot Wiley Post made the first solo round-the-world flight in 1933. His plane (below) was called *Winnie Mae*. In it he flew more than 25,000 km in 7 days, 18 hours and 49 minutes.

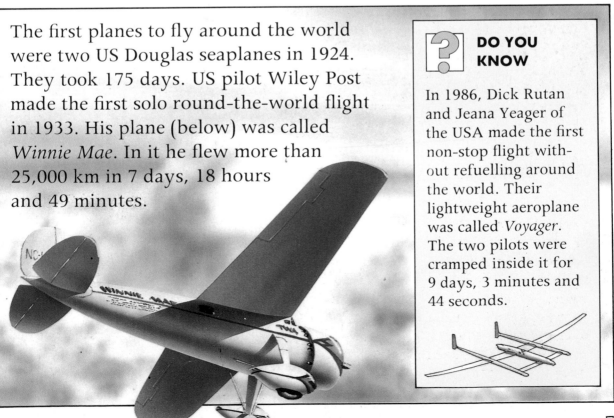

? DO YOU KNOW

In 1986, Dick Rutan and Jeana Yeager of the USA made the first non-stop flight without refuelling around the world. Their lightweight aeroplane was called *Voyager*. The two pilots were cramped inside it for 9 days, 3 minutes and 44 seconds.

How do aeroplanes stay in the air?

Planes can't fly without wings. These must have a special shape called an aerofoil, which is curved more above than below. Air flows faster over the aerofoil's curved upper surface than beneath it. This creates a force called lift, which enables the plane to fly.

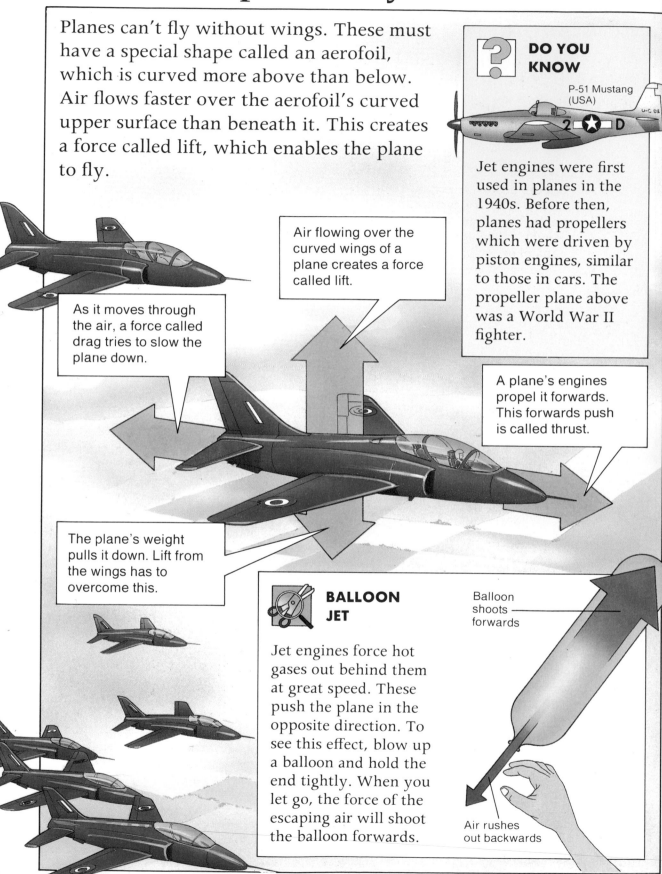

? DO YOU KNOW

P-51 Mustang (USA)

Jet engines were first used in planes in the 1940s. Before then, planes had propellers which were driven by piston engines, similar to those in cars. The propeller plane above was a World War II fighter.

Air flowing over the curved wings of a plane creates a force called lift.

As it moves through the air, a force called drag tries to slow the plane down.

A plane's engines propel it forwards. This forwards push is called thrust.

The plane's weight pulls it down. Lift from the wings has to overcome this.

BALLOON JET

Jet engines force hot gases out behind them at great speed. These push the plane in the opposite direction. To see this effect, blow up a balloon and hold the end tightly. When you let go, the force of the escaping air will shoot the balloon forwards.

Balloon shoots forwards

Air rushes out backwards

How do gliders stay in the air?

Gliders are planes without engines. Like all planes, though, a glider will fly only if it is moving fast enough to keep air flowing over its wings, and the lift is greater than its weight.

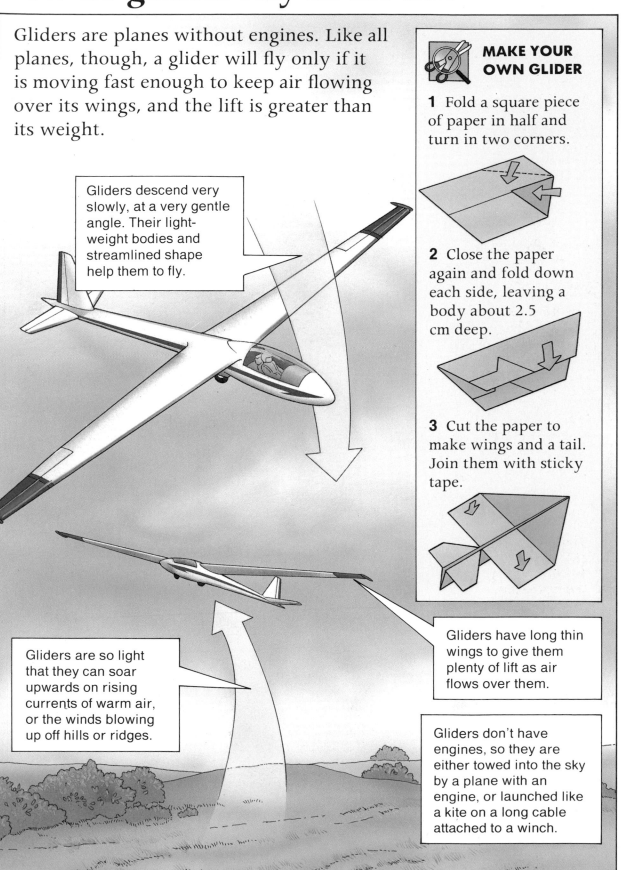

MAKE YOUR OWN GLIDER

1 Fold a square piece of paper in half and turn in two corners.

2 Close the paper again and fold down each side, leaving a body about 2.5 cm deep.

3 Cut the paper to make wings and a tail. Join them with sticky tape.

Gliders descend very slowly, at a very gentle angle. Their light-weight bodies and streamlined shape help them to fly.

Gliders have long thin wings to give them plenty of lift as air flows over them.

Gliders are so light that they can soar upwards on rising currents of warm air, or the winds blowing up off hills or ridges.

Gliders don't have engines, so they are either towed into the sky by a plane with an engine, or launched like a kite on a long cable attached to a winch.

How do helicopters fly?

Helicopters can hover in mid-air and fly in any direction – even backwards! Instead of wings they have spinning blades called rotors, which act as wings and propellers to give lift and thrust. Helicopter pilots control their craft by changing the pitch, or angle, at which the rotor blades spin through the air.

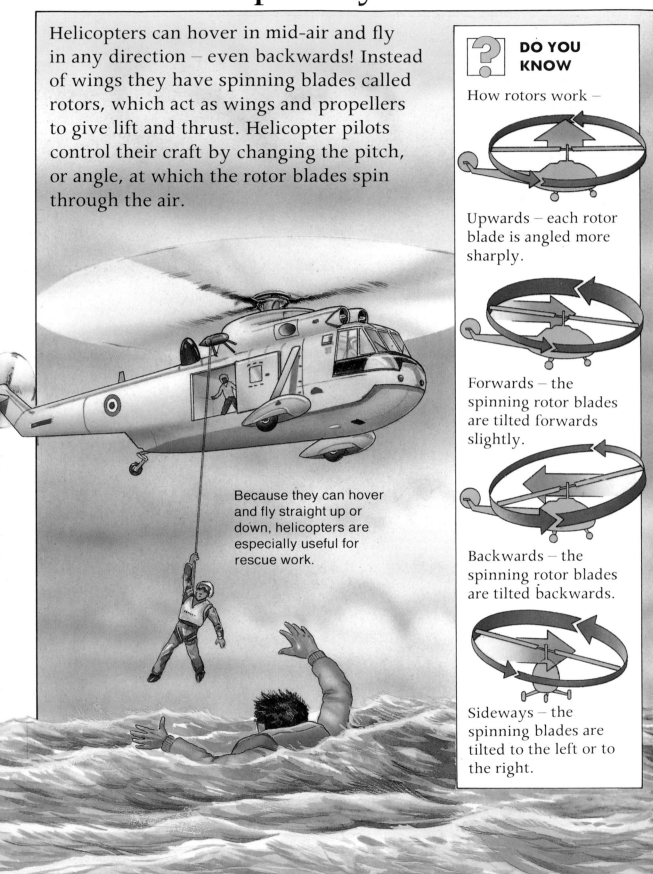

Because they can hover and fly straight up or down, helicopters are especially useful for rescue work.

? DO YOU KNOW

How rotors work –

Upwards – each rotor blade is angled more sharply.

Forwards – the spinning rotor blades are tilted forwards slightly.

Backwards – the spinning rotor blades are tilted backwards.

Sideways – the spinning blades are tilted to the left or to the right.

What are V/STOL jets?

V/STOL is short for 'vertical/short take-off and landing' (vertical means straight up or down). The jet engines of V/STOL planes have nozzles which can be angled downwards for take-off and landing. This allows V/STOL planes to fly straight up or down, just like helicopters do. V/STOL planes can also hover and fly backwards.

The Harrier's engine has four nozzles: When they point backwards, the jet thrust from them sends the plane forwards.

The Harrier (right and below) was the world's first successful V/STOL jet. It began test flights in the late 1960s.

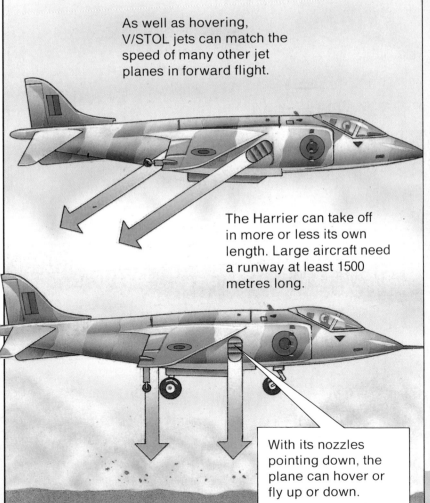

As well as hovering, V/STOL jets can match the speed of many other jet planes in forward flight.

The Harrier can take off in more or less its own length. Large aircraft need a runway at least 1500 metres long.

With its nozzles pointing down, the plane can hover or fly up or down.

? DO YOU KNOW

One of the earliest V/STOL planes was the Lockheed XFV-1. It was built for the US Navy and test flown in the early 1950s. As well as normal forward take-offs, it could take off and land vertically. Unlike modern V/STOLs, it was positioned tail down and nose up to do this – it was difficult to fly, however.

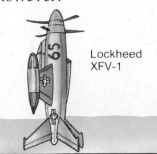

Lockheed XFV-1

Why do balloons fly?

Balloons fly because they are lighter than the air around them. Warm air is lighter than cold air, so a balloon filled with hot air will rise. Some balloons are filled with gases such as helium which are lighter than air.

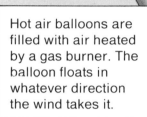

Hot air balloons are filled with air heated by a gas burner. The balloon floats in whatever direction the wind takes it.

To make the balloon descend, the pilot turns off the gas burner. This lets the air inside the balloon cool and get heavier.

 BALLOON FACTS

• The first balloon to carry living things was built in France by the two Montgolfier

brothers, and launched in 1783. A duck, a sheep and a rooster flew in the balloon's basket and landed safely after 8 minutes.

• The longest flight in a hot air balloon was made in 1991 by Richard Branson and Per Lindstrand of the UK. The two men flew 7672 km, from Japan to Canada.

• The highest flight for a balloon carrying people is 34,668 metres (1961).

Concorde – 15,240 metres

Mt Everest – 8848 metres

What are airships?

Airships are large balloons with engines. These give them enough power to fly in any direction, even into the wind.

The first successful airship flew in 1852. In the 1920s and 1930s, airships were used as long-distance airliners to carry passengers. Unfortunately they were filled with hydrogen gas, which catches fire easily, and several were destroyed in terrible fires.

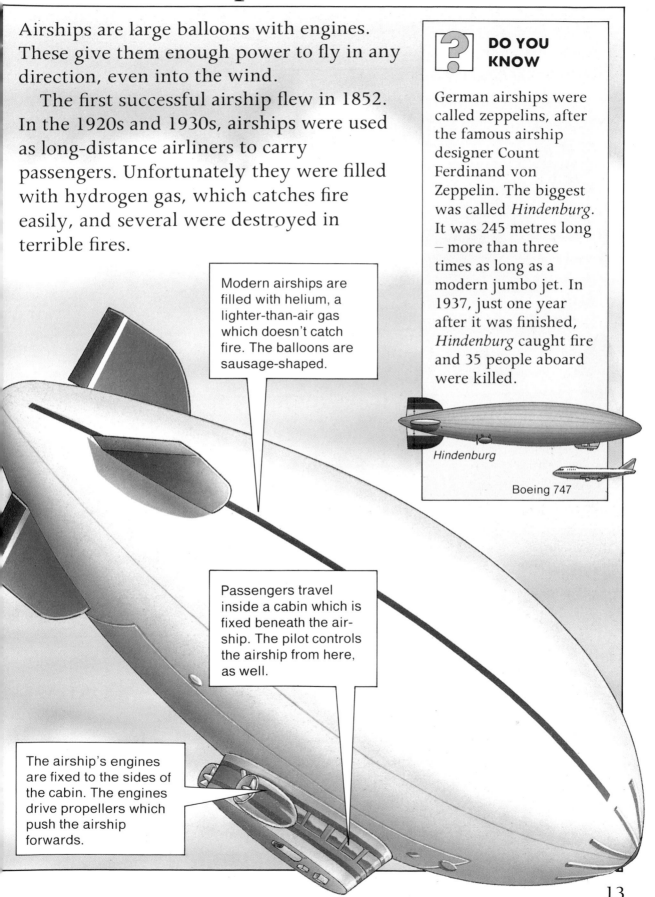

Hindenburg

Boeing 747

Modern airships are filled with helium, a lighter-than-air gas which doesn't catch fire. The balloons are sausage-shaped.

Passengers travel inside a cabin which is fixed beneath the airship. The pilot controls the airship from here, as well.

The airship's engines are fixed to the sides of the cabin. The engines drive propellers which push the airship forwards.

Which is the fastest car?

The world land speed record for a car is just over 1019 km/h – that's faster than many jet airliners can fly. It's held by the British car *Thrust 2*, which was propelled by the thrust from an aircraft jet engine. Because ordinary cars are powered by engines that drive the wheels round, they can't go as fast as jet or rocket cars. The top speed for a wheel-driven car is 691 km/h.

DO YOU KNOW

The wheel was invented about 6000 years ago. Before this, tree trunks were used as rollers to move heavy objects. Someone watching a roller turn probably thought of the wheel.

1 In 1899 the battery-powered *La Jamais Contente* (left) was the first car to go faster than 100 km/h.

2 Henry Segrave's Sunbeam car (below) set a record of 327.98 km/h in 1927.

3 The first car to go faster than 600 km/h was John Cobb's Railton (below), in 1947.

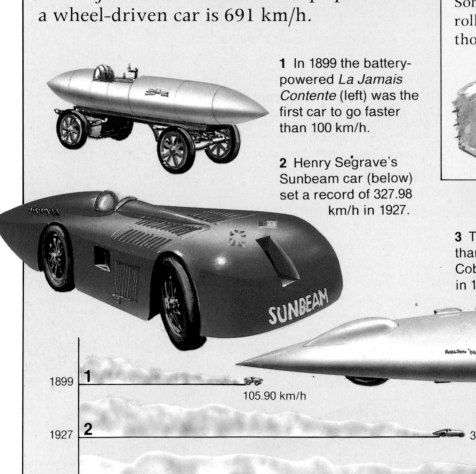

1899 **1**	105.90 km/h
1927 **2**	327.98 km/h
1947 **3**	
1964 **4**	
1970 **5**	
1983 **6**	

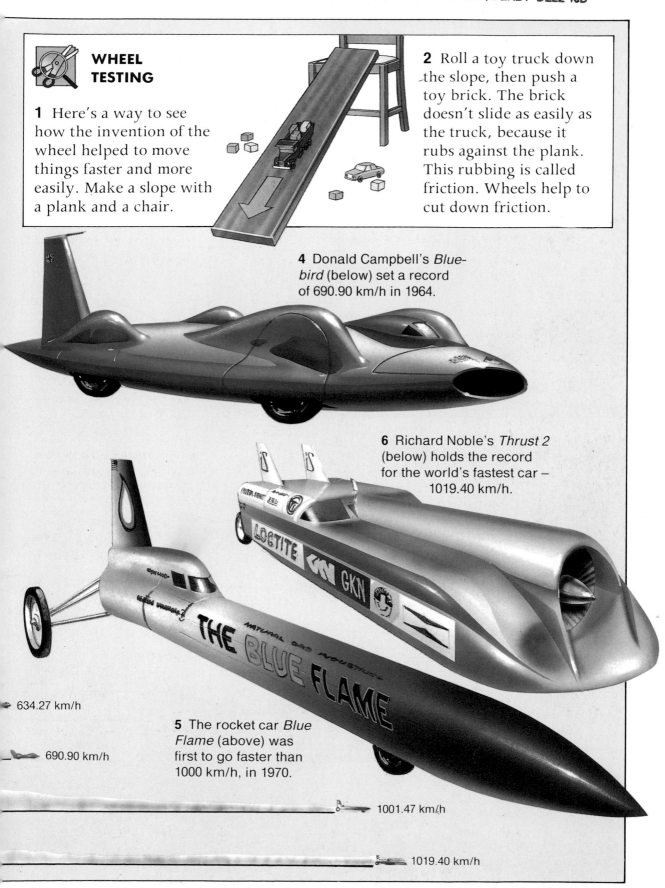

WHEEL TESTING

1 Here's a way to see how the invention of the wheel helped to move things faster and more easily. Make a slope with a plank and a chair.

2 Roll a toy truck down the slope, then push a toy brick. The brick doesn't slide as easily as the truck, because it rubs against the plank. This rubbing is called friction. Wheels help to cut down friction.

4 Donald Campbell's *Bluebird* (below) set a record of 690.90 km/h in 1964.

6 Richard Noble's *Thrust 2* (below) holds the record for the world's fastest car – 1019.40 km/h.

5 The rocket car *Blue Flame* (above) was first to go faster than 1000 km/h, in 1970.

634.27 km/h

690.90 km/h

1001.47 km/h

1019.40 km/h

15

Which is the most popular car?

More Volkswagen Beetles have been made than any other car – by the time European production stopped in 1978, over 20 million had been sold. The first Beetles were made in Germany in 1938. The German word *volkswagen* means 'people's car'.

? DO YOU KNOW

Ferrari cars have been sold at auction for over £6 million, making them the world's most expensive second-hand cars.

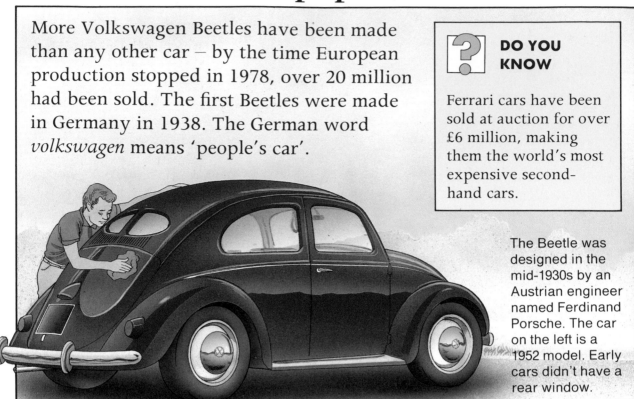

The Beetle was designed in the mid-1930s by an Austrian engineer named Ferdinand Porsche. The car on the left is a 1952 model. Early cars didn't have a rear window.

Which is the biggest car?

The biggest cars ever made were the Bugatti Royales of 1927. They were over 6.7 metres long and weighed 2.5 tonnes. Only a few Bugatti Royales were built – in 1986, a bidder at an auction paid over £4.5 million for one of them!

? DO YOU KNOW

The world's longest car is 30.5 metres long and has 26 wheels. This super-stretch limousine even has a waterbed and a mini-swimming pool.

Who invented the motor car?

The earliest powered road vehicle was built in 1769 and had a steam engine. But the first true motor car – with a petrol engine – was made by Karl Benz of Germany in 1885. Benz's car had three wheels and looked rather like a tricycle. Another German, Gottlieb Daimler, built a four-wheeled car in 1886.

ROAD TRAVEL FACTS

● The first crossroad traffic lights were put up in Detroit, USA, in 1919.

● The first motorway was opened in Italy in the 1920s.

● Reflecting cat's-eyes, to help drivers see the road at night, were invented in the year 1935.

1 The steam tractor below was the first powered road vehicle. It was built in 1769 by Nicolas-Joseph Cugnot of France to haul gun carriages.

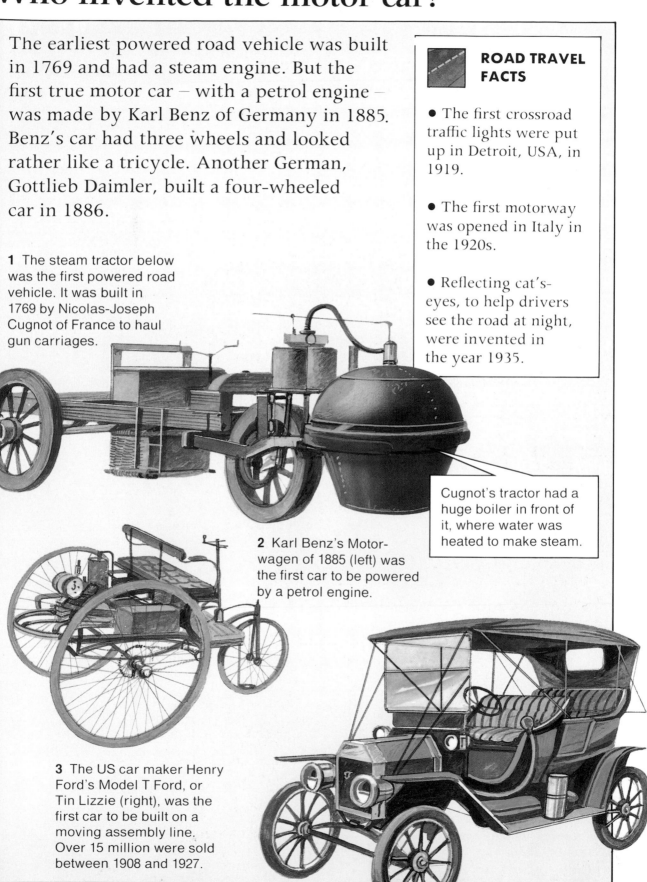

Cugnot's tractor had a huge boiler in front of it, where water was heated to make steam.

2 Karl Benz's Motor-wagen of 1885 (left) was the first car to be powered by a petrol engine.

3 The US car maker Henry Ford's Model T Ford, or Tin Lizzie (right), was the first car to be built on a moving assembly line. Over 15 million were sold between 1908 and 1927.

How are cars made?

Cars are put together in factories, on assembly lines. First, though, the body parts are cut and shaped from sheets of metal, by huge machines. The parts are then welded together to make the body. After this is painted, working parts such as the engine and gearbox are fitted. Finally, seats, windows and wheels are added, and the car is driven off for testing.

 CAR FACTS

- Licence plates were first put on cars in the 1890s.

- The first cars to be built on an assembly line were US Oldsmobiles, in 1901.

- Mechanical windscreen wipers first appeared on cars in 1910.

- The first cars with electric lights were made in 1912.

- Assembly lines with moving conveyor belts were introduced in 1913, by the US car maker Henry Ford.

- Tubeless car tyres were introduced in 1948.

- Robot welders were first used in car factories in 1970.

- North Americans own over 36% of the world's 480 million passenger cars.

The shell, or empty car body, is placed on the beginning of the assembly line.

In many factories, much of the welding and fitting is done by robots.

The assembly line is a conveyor system. A new car is made every few minutes.

How are cars tested?

Every newly made car is tested at the factory to make sure it works properly. All the parts are checked, and the finished car is passed by an inspector. New car designs are tested even more thoroughly, and go through months of trials before production begins. They are always crash-tested to see how strong and safe they are.

DO YOU KNOW

In Britain, the first cars were banned from going faster than 6 km/h. Someone had to walk in front with a red flag to warn people that a car was coming.

To see what happens in a crash, a test car with a dummy driver is driven into a wall. This helps people to design safer cars.

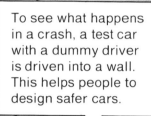

Speed track tests show car makers how well the engine works, how fast the car can go, and how safe it is travelling at high speed.

LAWS OF MOTION

1 If a car hits something, the passengers are thrown forwards. If they aren't wearing seat belts, they may even be flung out of the car. This is because things that are already moving tend to keep going – scientists call this effect inertia. Here's a way to see inertia in action for yourself.

2 Load a toy truck with toy bricks. Push the truck so that it crashes into something. The truck stops, but inertia makes the bricks keep on moving.

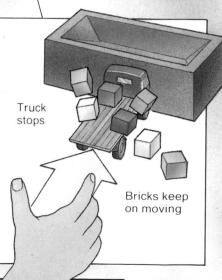

Truck stops

Bricks keep on moving

Which is the world's longest road race?

First held in 1923, France's Le Mans race lasts for 24 hours and covers a distance of about 5300 km. The winner is the car that travels farthest in 24 hours.

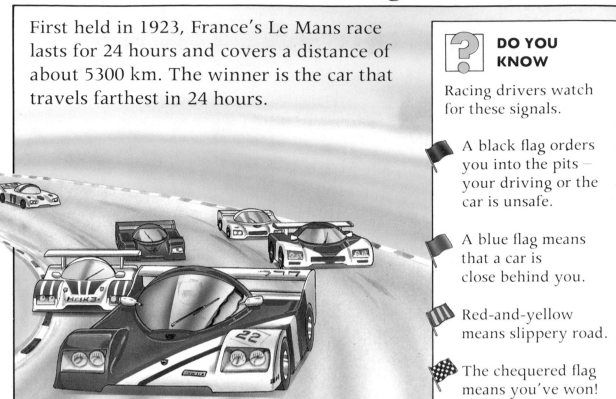

? DO YOU KNOW

Racing drivers watch for these signals.

A black flag orders you into the pits – your driving or the car is unsafe.

A blue flag means that a car is close behind you.

Red-and-yellow means slippery road.

The chequered flag means you've won!

Where is the world's longest road?

The Pan-American Highway is the world's longest road system. It covers 47,500 km, East-West and North-South. It starts at the northern border of Mexico (USA) and stretches almost to the tip of South America.

? DO YOU KNOW

Roads are made from layers of stones, and concrete or asphalt (bitumen). The road surface is cambered, or curved, so rain drains off it.

Surface – concrete or asphalt

Base – concrete. stone or asphalt

Road bed – rock or soil

What is a road train?

Road trains are long truck-trailer combinations – a large powerful truck pulling two or more big trailers loaded with cargo. They are often used in parts of a country where there are no railways. In Australia, for example, road trains are often used to transport animals from remote sheep or cattle farms.

? DO YOU KNOW

The wagons used by early North American settlers were pulled by oxen, mules or horses. One wagon carried everything a family owned. Wagons travelled in a line, forming a wagon train.

When were bicycles invented?

The earliest bicycles, called dandy-horses, appeared in the 1790s. They didn't have pedals, and riders pushed themselves along with their feet. The first pedal bicycle was made by a Scot called Kirkpatrick Macmillan in 1839. The first modern-looking bicycle was the *vélocipède* made by Pierre Michaux of France in 1861.

1 Dandy-horses (right) were invented in France in the 1790s. Kicking themselves along with their feet, riders could reach speeds of 15 km/h.

2 The *vélocipède* (below), or bone-shaker, was invented in 1861. It was the first bicycle with a brake. It didn't have a chain or gears, though – the pedals turned the front wheel.

3 The penny-farthing (above) was invented in 1870. To climb on, riders used a small step just above the back wheel. Once moving, they could reach speeds of more than 30 km/h.

4 The first bicycle with pedals linked by a chain to the back wheel appeared in the 1880s. Gears were invented in the 1900s – modern bicycles (right) can have anything from 3 to 21 of them.
    Gears make cycling less hard work. In low gear, the rear wheel turns more slowly than the pedals, giving more power for starts and hills. In high gear, the wheels turn much faster than the pedals.

Which is the fastest motorbike?

The Kawasaki ZZ-R1100 (below) is one of the world's fastest road bikes. In tests, this Japanese motorbike has done more than 280 km/h. Racing bikes can go even faster, however, and reach speeds greater than 300 km/h.

The first motorbike with a petrol engine was called the *Einspur*. It was made in Germany in 1885, by Gottlieb Daimler and Wilhelm Maybach.

MOTORBIKE FACTS

● The *Einspur* (below) was the first motorbike. Apart from its engine, it was made out of wood. Its top speed was 19 km/h.

● By the 1930s, motorbikes could travel faster than 200 km/h.

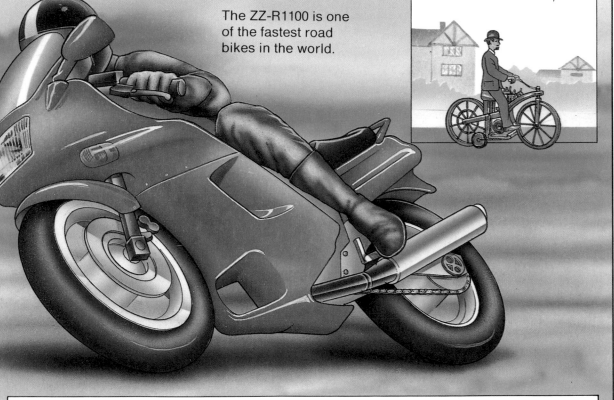

The ZZ-R1100 is one of the fastest road bikes in the world.

 TEST DRIVE BALL BEARINGS

1 Inside the wheels of bikes and cars are little metal balls called bearings, which help the wheels to spin round smoothly.

2 Here's a way to see how bearings work. Put some marbles in the rim of an empty tin. Place a book on top and spin it gently.

3 Now try spinning the book without the marbles!

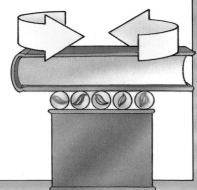

Who built the first locomotive?

The world's first working steam locomotive was built by Richard Trevithick of England. It made its first journey in February 1804, along the rails of a Welsh mine track.

The first public railway, the Stockton and Darlington Railway in north-east England, opened in 1825. The steam locomotive below is the one that pulled the line's first train. It was called *Locomotion* and it was designed by George Stephenson.

STEAM FACTS

● Richard Trevithick's 1804 steam locomotive (above) covered nearly 15 km on its first journey, at a speed of 8 km/h.

● In 1829, George Stephenson's new locomotive *Rocket* achieved a top speed of 47 km/h.

● The first French steam locomotive was built by Marc Séguin in 1829.

● The first US-built locomotive, Peter Cooper's *Tom Thumb*, had its first run on 25 August 1830.

On its first run in 1825, Stephenson's *Locomotion* hauled the owner's coach, 11 coal wagons, a wagon of flour, 20 wagons of guests and workmen, plus an extra 300 people who climbed on for the ride. It averaged 13 km/h, but reached 24 km/h downhill.

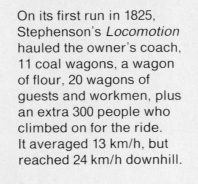

Which was the fastest steam train?

The fastest steam train was pulled by the British locomotive *Mallard*. In 1938 it reached nearly 203 km/h, travelling slightly downhill. *Mallard* was pulling seven coaches weighing over 240 tonnes.

DO YOU KNOW

Trainspotters know a locomotive's type by the arrangement of its wheels. *Mallard* was a 4-6-2 Pacific class engine. 4-6-2 means it had 4 front wheels, 6 driving wheels, and 2 rear wheels. Two other locomotive classes are shown below.

Atlantic

Pacific

Mountain

Which is the fastest electric train?

The fastest electric train is the French TGV, which set a record of 515 km/h in 1990. West Germany's InterCity Express (ICE) can do 400 km/h, while Britain's Intercity 225 can reach 225 km/h.

DO YOU KNOW

France's TGV (*Train à Grande Vitesse*) speeds the 425 kilometres from Paris to Lyon in just 2 hours – that's over 200 km/h.

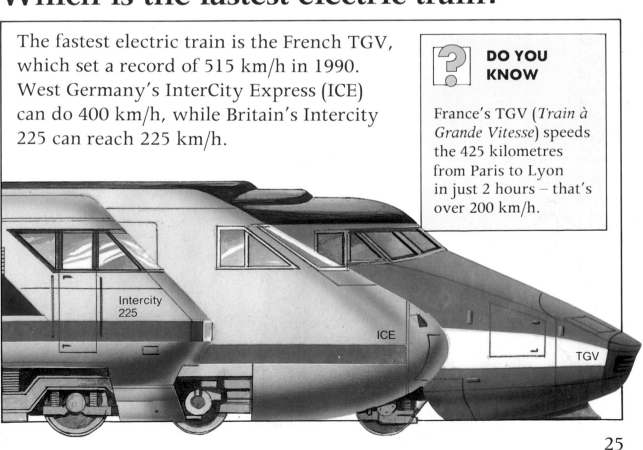

Intercity 225

ICE

TGV

Where is the world's longest railway?

The longest railway in the world is the Trans-Siberian line, which is 9438 km long. It runs from Moscow, in western Russia, across the frozen plains and forests of Siberia to Nakhodka, in eastern Russia. The whole journey takes eight days.

RAILWAY FACTS

● The longest straight line of track in the world runs for 478 km across the Nullarbor Plain of Western and South Australia.

● Gauge is the distance between the rails of a railway track. Railways can be standard, narrow or broad gauge. Standard gauge is just over 1.4 metres.

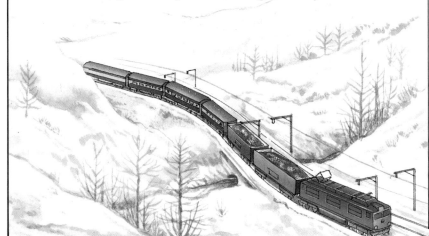

Where is the world's highest railway?

The world's highest standard-gauge railway is in South America, where a line of the Peruvian State Railways climbs to 4817 metres in the Andes. This is higher than Mont Blanc, the highest peak in the European Alps.

? DO YOU KNOW

The first railway to cross a continent was built across the USA in 1863–69. It was 2775 km long.

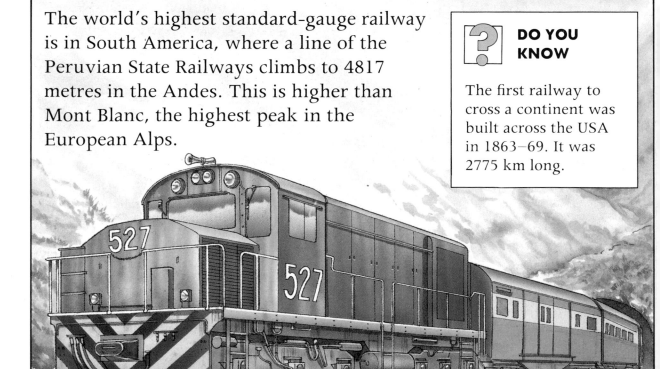

What are monorails?

Mono means one, and monorails are trains that run on one rail, not two. The rail is set on a track which is usually well above the ground. Some monorail trains straddle the track and travel along the top of it. Others hang beneath the track. Monorails have been built in cities throughout the world, to carry people above streets busy with traffic. Others carry visitors through theme parks.

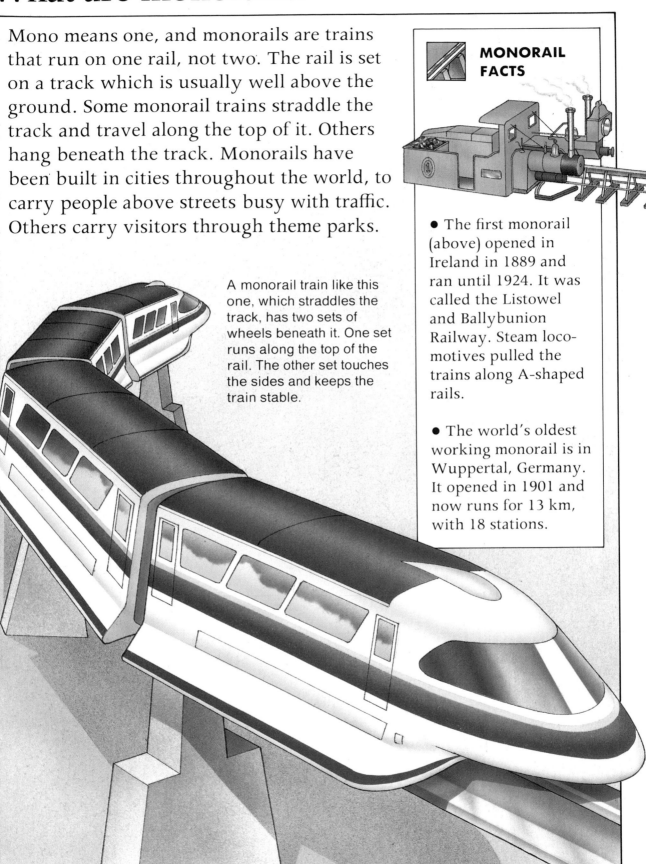

MONORAIL FACTS

● The first monorail (above) opened in Ireland in 1889 and ran until 1924. It was called the Listowel and Ballybunion Railway. Steam locomotives pulled the trains along A-shaped rails.

● The world's oldest working monorail is in Wuppertal, Germany. It opened in 1901 and now runs for 13 km, with 18 stations.

A monorail train like this one, which straddles the track, has two sets of wheels beneath it. One set runs along the top of the rail. The other set touches the sides and keeps the train stable.

Which are the biggest ships?

The biggest ships in the world today are cargo vessels such as oil tankers. These giant ships can be more than a third of a kilometre long and weigh around 400,000 tonnes.

The world's biggest passenger ship is a Norwegian cruise liner, the *Norway*. This ship is a rebuilt version of the 1961 transatlantic liner *SS France*, with two extra decks. It is just over 315.5 metres long.

? DO YOU KNOW

Some tankers are so huge that the crew use bicycles to get about the deck. A big tanker can take 20 minutes, and 8 km, to stop!

The *Queen Elizabeth 2* (right) is one of the world's largest passenger liners. It is 294 metres long and weighs 67,000 tonnes. The 83,000-tonne *Queen Elizabeth* was the largest passenger ship ever built.

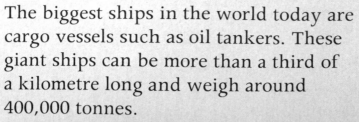

The world's longest aircraft carrier is the US Navy's *Enterprise* (below), at 336 metres. The US Navy's Nimitz class carriers are shorter, but heavier. Completed in 1960, *Enterprise* was the first nuclear-powered aircraft carrier.

WHY DO SHIPS FLOAT?

Ships only float if they weigh less than the amount of water they displace, or push aside.

1 You can see how this works by half-filling a bowl with water. Mark

the water level on the side of the bowl. Use a tin or plastic food container for a ship, and put it into the water.

2 Now pour a little sand into your 'ship' – it will sink farther into the water. As it does, it displaces some of the water – look at your original water level mark. If you overload your 'ship' with sand it will sink.

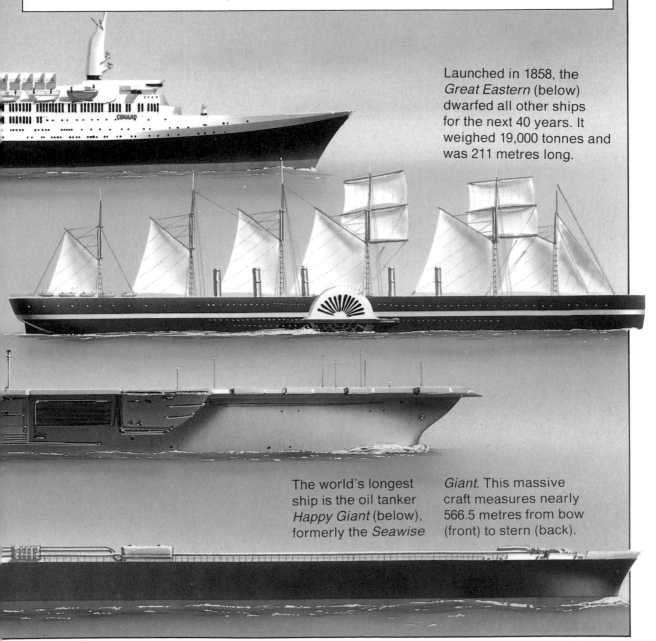

Launched in 1858, the *Great Eastern* (below) dwarfed all other ships for the next 40 years. It weighed 19,000 tonnes and was 211 metres long.

The world's longest ship is the oil tanker *Happy Giant* (below), formerly the *Seawise Giant*. This massive craft measures nearly 566.5 metres from bow (front) to stern (back).

What were the first boats like?

People have been building and sailing boats for many thousands of years. The earliest and most simple type of boat was a flat raft made by lashing logs together. People also made canoes called dug-outs, using fire and axes to hollow out tree trunks. Another early type of boat is called a coracle. These small round boats were made by stretching animal skins over a lightweight wooden framework.

DO YOU KNOW

In 1970, a Norwegian named Thor Heyerdahl sailed a copy of an Ancient Egyptian reed boat across the Atlantic Ocean, in an attempt to prove that the Egyptians introduced reed boats to South America.

One of the earliest types of boat was a log raft (right). It was sturdy enough for crossing a river or a lake, but not for setting out to sea.

In the South Pacific, outrigger canoes like the one below have been used for ocean crossings for thousands of years.

Egyptian wall paintings made over 6000 years ago show rafts like the one below. The Ancient Egyptians built their rafts by lashing together bundles of a reed-like plant called papyrus.

Outrigger

Dug-out canoe

How fast could sailing ships travel?

The fastest sailing ships were the clippers of the mid-1800s. These graceful cargo ships were designed for speed, with long sleek bodies and many sails. In a strong wind, with all sails set, they could travel at over 35 km/h. By the late 1800s, however, clippers had been overtaken by faster ships, which were powered by steam engines.

DO YOU KNOW

In 1866, the two clippers *Taeping* and *Ariel* raced from China to Britain in 99 days, and arrived only 20 minutes apart!

A typical clipper had three masts – the front one was called the foremast, the middle one was the mainmast, and the rear one was the mizzenmast. As many as 35 square sails could be set.

Mainmast

Mizzen-mast

Foremast

SAILING FACTS

• A clipper of the 1800s could cross the Atlantic in 12 days. The record crossing time for a modern passenger liner is just under 3½ days.

• The biggest sailing ships of the 1800s were called windjammers. The largest, the *Preussen*, weighed 5000 tonnes and had five masts.

• The longest distance covered under sail in one day was claimed as 748 km, by the captain of the clipper *Champion of the Seas* in 1854.

• The highest speed reached by any sailing craft is nearly 83 km/h, by a sailboard in 1991.

How do paddle-steamers work?

As their name suggests, these boats are powered by paddles and steam. The paddles are wide boards set into a large wheel, which is driven by a steam engine. As the wheel turns into the water, the paddles push against it. This makes the boat move. The earliest paddle-steamers had two wheels – one on either side of the centre of the boat. Nowadays, most have a single large wheel at the back.

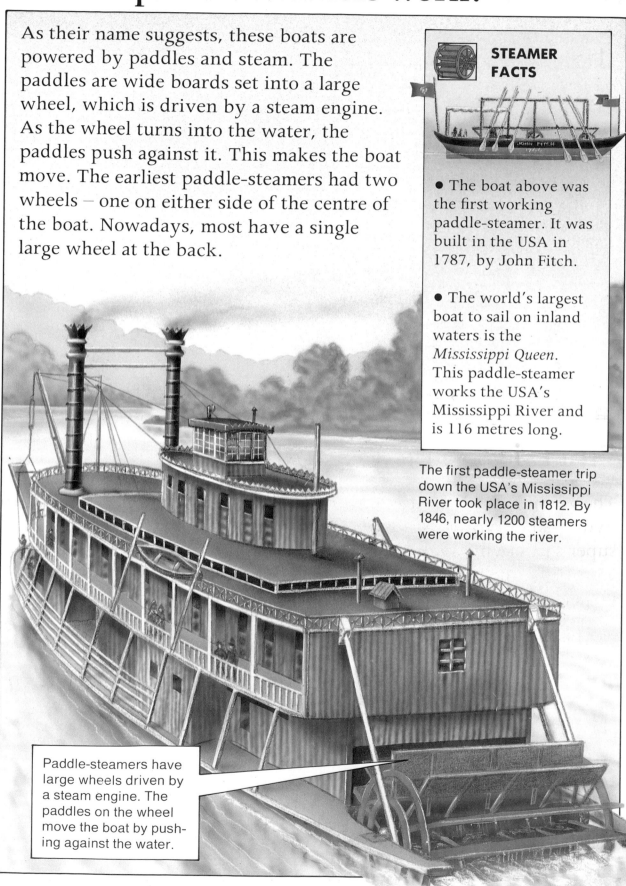

STEAMER FACTS

● The boat above was the first working paddle-steamer. It was built in the USA in 1787, by John Fitch.

● The world's largest boat to sail on inland waters is the *Mississippi Queen*. This paddle-steamer works the USA's Mississippi River and is 116 metres long.

The first paddle-steamer trip down the USA's Mississippi River took place in 1812. By 1846, nearly 1200 steamers were working the river.

Paddle-steamers have large wheels driven by a steam engine. The paddles on the wheel move the boat by pushing against the water.

Who first sailed solo around the world?

The first person to sail alone around the world was Joshua Slocum in 1895-98. His yacht, *Spray*, was only 11.5 metres long. The first non-stop solo round-the-world voyage was made by Robin Knox-Johnston in 1968-69. He spent 312 days at sea in his boat *Suhaili*.

Which is the fastest boat?

The world's fastest boat is Ken Warby's hydroplane *Spirit of Australia*. In 1977, this super-fast machine roared across a lake at 556 km/h. The fastest speed reached by a powerboat is just over 368 km/h.

Hydroplanes are designed to skim over the surface of the water in almost the same way as a flat stone does when thrown.

How do hovercraft hover?

Hovercraft skim across the surface of the water or the land on a cushion of air. Fans blow air downwards, where it is trapped inside the flexible, or bendy, skirt which surrounds the hovercraft. Floating on this trapped cushion of air, the hovercraft is driven along by aircraft-type propellers.

DO YOU KNOW

The world hovercraft speed record is held by the US Navy's SES-100B. This test craft reached a speed of 170 km/h in 1980.

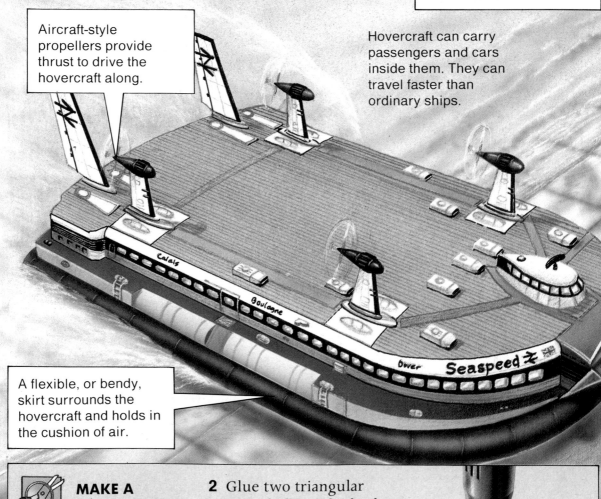

Aircraft-style propellers provide thrust to drive the hovercraft along.

Hovercraft can carry passengers and cars inside them. They can travel faster than ordinary ships.

A flexible, or bendy, skirt surrounds the hovercraft and holds in the cushion of air.

 MAKE A HOVERCRAFT

1 Ask an adult to help you cut a hovercraft shape, with a hole about 5 cm across in the middle, out of a piece of polystyrene tile.

2 Glue two triangular pieces of tile on the back as rudders.

3 Put your hovercraft on a flat dry surface and use a hair dryer to blow air through the hole to make it float.

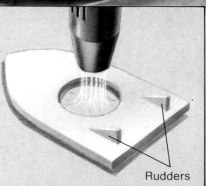

Rudders

What is a hydrofoil?

A hydrofoil is a boat whose hull, or body, can lift above the water when it is travelling at speed. Most have two underwater wings called foils – one at the bow, or front, and one at the stern, or rear. As it builds up speed, the hydrofoil rises up on its foils and can skim over the water at speeds of 55 to 100 km/h.

1 When it isn't travelling at speed, a hydrofoil floats in the water just like any other boat (below).

2 As the hydrofoil gathers speed (right), it rises higher out of the water on its foils.

Lift is created as water rushes over the curved upper surface of the boat's foils.

Foils have a curved upper surface and work like aircraft wings to create lift.

How deep can submarines dive?

Most submarines cruise below the surface of the water at a depth of about 150 metres. Few can dive below 450 metres. This is because water has pressure, or push, which increases with depth. Deep below the surface of the ocean, the water pressure is enough to squash the steel hull of the average submarine as flat as a pancake!

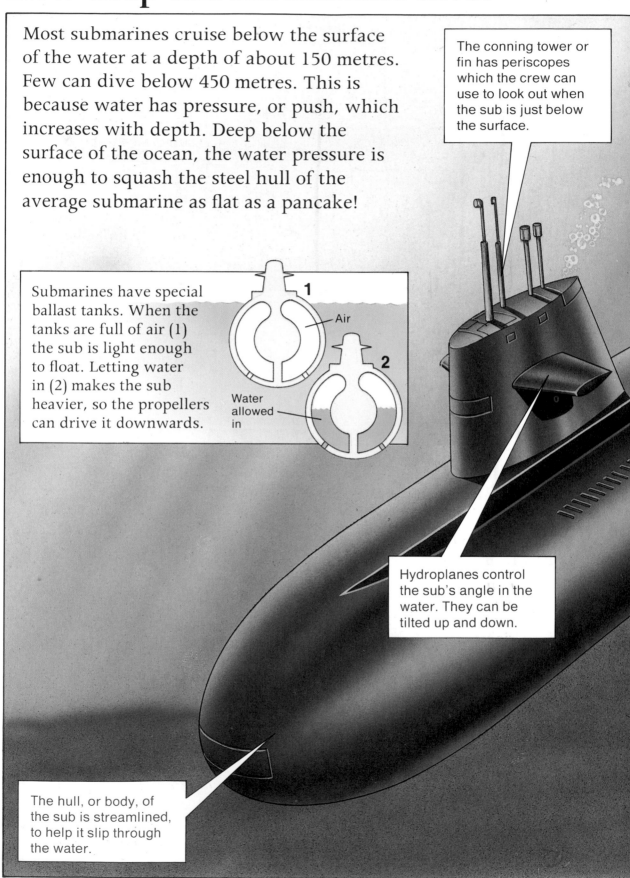

The conning tower or fin has periscopes which the crew can use to look out when the sub is just below the surface.

Submarines have special ballast tanks. When the tanks are full of air (1) the sub is light enough to float. Letting water in (2) makes the sub heavier, so the propellers can drive it downwards.

1

Air

2

Water allowed in

Hydroplanes control the sub's angle in the water. They can be tilted up and down.

The hull, or body, of the sub is streamlined, to help it slip through the water.

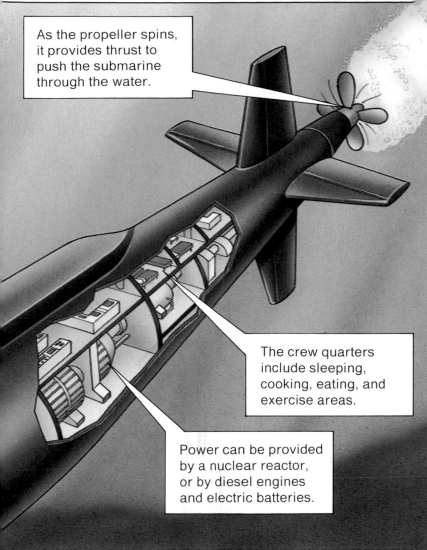

As the propeller spins, it provides thrust to push the submarine through the water.

The crew quarters include sleeping, cooking, eating, and exercise areas.

Power can be provided by a nuclear reactor, or by diesel engines and electric batteries.

 SUBMARINE FACTS

SUBMARINE FACTS

- The tiny *Turtle* (below) was the first submarine to be used in battle. In 1776, during the American War of Independence, it was used to try to mine a British ship in New York Harbor, but failed. One person sat inside and turned the propeller by hand to push it along.

Turtle

- The *Resurgam* (below) was built in 1879 and had a steam engine. Unfortunately, it sank with its crew on board.

Resurgam

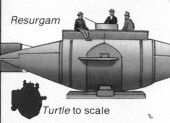

Turtle to scale

- The US inventor John P. Holland made the first successful submarine in 1897. Petrol engines drove it on the surface. Underwater it ran on battery-driven motors.

 DO YOU KNOW

The *Trieste* (right) is a special kind of submarine called a bathyscaphe, which can cope with the enormous pressure of deep water. In 1960 it dived nearly 11,000 metres into the deepest part of the Pacific Ocean. The cabin is in the ball underneath.

What will future transport be like?

One of the main changes in transport will be in the fuel that's used. Nowadays, most vehicles get power from burning petrol in an engine. But petrol is made from oil, and the world's oil reserves are running out fast. Other, cleaner fuels must be found, since burning petrol also produces gases which pollute, or dirty, the air.

Maglev trains are a new and very fast type of intercity transport. They float above the track on an invisible magnetic field.

New V/STOL designs include planes whose rotors tilt up for vertical take-off and landing, and forwards for normal flight.

The Sun's energy can be collected by special panels and used to make electricity to power small road vehicles and aircraft.

Useful words

Fuselage   The body of an aeroplane.

Jet engine   An engine in which fuel and oxygen (from air) are burnt to make a jet of hot gases. The gases shoot backwards out of the engine, producing thrust and propelling the machine forwards.

Lift   The force that keeps an aircraft airborne. Air has pressure, or push, and lift is created by the difference in air-pressure above and below the aircraft's wings. These must have a special shape called an aerofoil, which is curved more above than below. The air flowing over an aerofoil's curved upper surface moves faster, and has less pressure, than the air flowing beneath it. Water flowing over the curved foils of a hydrofoil creates lift in the same way.

Locomotive   The part of a train which contains the engines and pulls the carriages.

Petrol engine   An engine in which petrol and air are burnt, producing hot gases. The gases force a piston up and down a cylinder inside the engine. A connecting rod and crankshaft then change this up-and-down movement to circular movement – the wheels go round and the car or other machine moves. Most car engines have four to six cylinders.

Propel   Another word for push.

Rotor   The rotating, or spinning, part of a machine. The rotor of a helicopter consists of the spinning blades which give it lift.

Steam engine   An engine in which fuel such as coal or wood is burnt to heat water in a boiler. When the water boils, it turns into steam, which is used to drive a piston backwards and forwards. Connecting rods and a crankshaft attached to the piston then change this back-and-forth movement into circular movement – the wheels go round and the locomotive or other machine moves.

Thrust   The force that pushes a machine forwards. Modern aircraft are given thrust by their jet engines. The spinning propeller of a ship or submarine also creates thrust.

V/STOL   Short for 'vertical/short take-off and landing'.

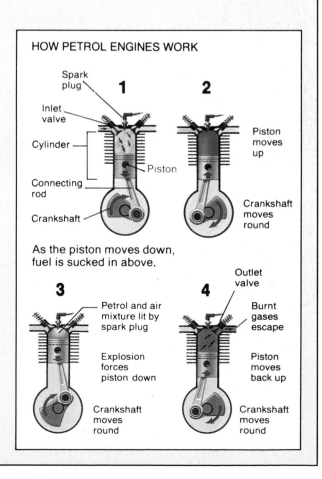

HOW PETROL ENGINES WORK

Spark plug

Inlet valve

Cylinder

Connecting rod

Crankshaft

Piston

1   **2**

Piston moves up

Crankshaft moves round

As the piston moves down, fuel is sucked in above.

3   **4**

Petrol and air mixture lit by spark plug

Explosion forces piston down

Crankshaft moves round

Outlet valve

Burnt gases escape

Piston moves back up

Crankshaft moves round

Index

A
aerofoil 8
aircraft 4–13
Antonov An-225 6

B
balloon 12, 13
Bell X-1 4
Bell X-2 5
Benz, Karl 17
bicycle 22
Blériot monoplane 5
Bluebird 15
Blue Flame 15
boat 30–33, 35
Boeing 747 6, 7
Bugatti Royale 16

C
Campbell, Donald 15
car 14–20
clipper 31
Concorde 4–5
conning tower 36
Cooper, Peter 24
coracle 30
Cugnot, Nicolas-J. 17

D
Daimler, Gottlieb 17, 23
dandy-horse 22
Douglas Skyrocket 5
drag 8

E
Einspur 23
engine 8, 11, 14, 17, 39
Enterprise 28–29

F
Ferrari 16
Fitch, John 32
Flyer No. 1 7
foil 35
Ford, Henry 17, 18
friction 15
fuselage 6, 39

G
gears 22
glider 9
Great Eastern 29

H
Happy Giant 28–29
Harrier 11
helicopter 10

Heyerdahl, Thor 30
Hindenburg 13
Holland, John P. 37
hovercraft 34
hydrofoil 35
hydroplane 33

I
ICE 25
inertia 19
Intercity 225 25

J
jet car 14–15
jet engine 6, 8, 11, 14, 39
jet plane 4–5, 6, 8, 11

K
Kawasaki ZZ-R1100 23
Knox-Johnston, Robin 33

L
La Jamais Contente 14
Le Mans 20
lift 8, 9, 10, 35, 39
Listowel and Ballybunion
    Railway 27
Lockheed SR-71A 4
Lockheed XFV-1 11
Locomotion 24
locomotive 24, 25, 39

M
Mach 4, 5
Macmillan, Kirkpatrick 22
Magellan, Ferdinand 33
Maglev train 38
Mallard 25
Maybach, Wilhelm 23
Michaux, Pierre 22
Model T Ford 17
monorail 27
Montgolfier brothers 12
motorbike 23
Motorwagen 17

O
oil tanker 28–29
outrigger canoe 30

P
P-51 Mustang 8
paddle-steamer 32
Pan-American Highway 20
penny-farthing 22
petrol engine 17, 38, 39

Porsche, Ferdinand 16
Post, Wiley 7
propeller 8, 13, 34, 37

Q
Queen Elizabeth 2 28–29

R
Railton 14
Resurgam 37
road train 21
Rocket 24
rotor 10, 38, 39

S
sailboard 31
Santos-Dumont, Alberto 5
Seawise Giant 28–29
Segrave, Henry 14
Séguin, Marc 24
ship 28–29, 31
Slocum, Joshua 33
Spirit of Australia 33
SR-71A Blackbird 5
steam engine 17, 24, 25, 32, 39
Stephenson, George 24
submarine 36–37
Sunbeam 14

T
TGV 25
thrust 8, 10, 34, 37, 39
Thrust 2 14, 15
Tour de France 22
train 24–27
Trans-Siberian railway 26
Trevithick, Richard 24
Trieste 37
Turtle 37

V
vélocipède 22
Volkswagen Beetle 16
Voyager 7
V/STOL 11, 38, 39

W
Wharby, Ken 33
Winnie Mae 7
Wright, Orville and Wilbur 7

X
X-15 4

Z
zeppelin 13